YOU, TOO, CAN MAKE MONEY SELLING "GOOD JUNK" !

(An easy and quick guide to starting
a business selling **"Good Junk"**)

By
Linda M. LaRock

Editor
Michael Carpenter

INTRODUCTION

This book is not about selling fine antiques. It's about how you can make money selling the ordinary, everyday stuff you can find at yard sales and flea markets. It may not make you wealthy, but you can make money and have some fun, too. Everyone is looking for an easy, fast way to make extra money. What if I could show you how to enjoy your hobby and make money? I can! Seven years ago I found a way to do exactly that.

Almost every day someone asks me "How did you get started?" In this book, I will share with you some common sense, easy-to-read and practical information so that you too can start making money. We will help you to sell on the Internet, dealer to dealer, and from your backyard shop or garage.

So let's get started. If you can dream it... you can do it!

TABLE OF CONTENTS

CHAPTER 1: What Is "Good Junk"

I call it " Good Junk." It's really about selling a memory. It's the china that your Mother always served Thanksgiving dinner on. It's the "Bert and Ernie" finger puppets that your daughter entertained the church congregation with on Easter Sunday...during mass! It's the crisp, lacy crocheted doily that your Aunt Mary kept on her coffee table. It could be anything. . . well, almost anything!

Sometimes it's a newer item, like a wedding gift that was never used or a collectible figurine the owner no longer is crazy about. Often it's a quality judgement call. Does it have eye appeal like a glass bowl with curvy lines or an unusual color. Does it evoke strong memories like an old Elvis record? Perhaps it's just really cute or something you never saw before.

Selling junk is a gamble. You pay a dollar or two in hopes of making $20., $30., $50. or more. It's fun...it's entertaining... and it can be profitable for you.

A few years ago, I walked into a local antique shop and was instantly attracted to a perfume bottle from the 1960's. It was an April Showers cutie wearing her Hawaiian skirt and holding an umbrella. I knew she would easily sell for $30., so I gladly paid the dealer the asking price of $7. A week later she sold on " eBay" for more than $320.!

On another buying day, I went to my favorite flea market and found a lovely old pie bird. Pie birds are little figurines that were used to allow steam to escape from a pie while it was baking. This one was not marked by the manufacturer, but I knew they often sell for more than $40. I paid the asking price of $10. Canadian (about $6. in American money). I did not know she was a " Josef Original" in an unusual color. I sold her for more than $300.! Not every day produces such great results, but you will have enough really good days to offset the bad ones.

"Good Junk" really can be almost anything used. You need to think about what you might buy used. How about an L.L.Bean wool sweater... a Snow Baby figurine...a Fire King Jadite coffee mug? See how easy this can be?

Did you ever wonder who sells the "Good Junk?" Who are the "eBayers"...the "Cybersellers"? We are people who want extra income. We are people tired of traditional careers. We are the housewives, the disabled, the retired, and the passionate antiquers. Our common ground is our interest in poking around garage sales, flea markets and yard sales. And, as long as we are there doing what we enjoy doing, we try to make some money by buying something for a low price and selling it for a higher price.

My personal story began with a disabling back injury, compounded with an impending divorce. I needed to make a living that did not require a lot of scheduled work hours. I asked myself two key questions. "How can I stop working 40 hours a week at a traditional job yet earn enough money to support myself?" and "What do I know how to do?"

I was in a wonderful position to simplify my life. I had a passion for antique shops, auctions and for the people who sold these types of items. I decided to take a risk. I stopped working forty hours a week at a "regular" job, started a business in my home and began selling my "Good Junk" online. I had one goal in mind --- to provide a good product to my customers at a fair price, while providing excellent customer service.

This formula has worked to provide me with the income I need.

You can do it, too!

CHAPTER 2: Can You Make Money Selling "Good Junk"?

The answer is ... YES!

Ask yourself a few questions. Are you drawn to antique shops, auctions and thrift stores? Do you love old things? Do you walk into a department store and find yourself instinctively looking at the better quality merchandise that catch your eye? Are you collecting anything? Do you love to shop? Do you like to find out the history of the little items that attract your attention? Can you spend a few hours surfing the Internet?

If your answer is "YES" to any of these questions, then you definitely can make money selling " Good Junk." It's fun. It's a passion. It's a way of life.

Buying and reselling can become an all-consuming hobby; one that not only earns money, but that is also a wonderful way to meet people. It's a great occupation for all types of people. Loners, introverts and extroverts can do well selling "Good Junk." It's a great hobby for couples, too. You can travel and deduct a portion of your expenses from your income.

You need to decide how much money you want to earn monthly. You should also decide how much time you can devote to your new business. Some "Good Junk" dealers sell just enough to cover the cost of their hobby, other dealers do it as a part time income, while some " power sellers" sell full time. The more items you offer for sale or auction, the more potential income you will generate.

The best thing about selling online is that your office is in your home. Your store can be open 24 hours a day, seven days a week (if you sell online). You can be making money even if you are asleep or on vacation!

Now, the next question is.......... What should you sell?

Perhaps a better question is ...What do you like? You can specialize in one item, i.e., Fenton glass, trading cards or used clothing. Some sellers are experts in one area. Some of us are opportunists. We buy and sell a variety of goods depending on what's available at the moment; antiques, used collectibles, newer items and some junky guesses. My method has always been to buy whatever no one else is buying on a given day. For example, if you attend a furniture auction, perhaps you will find that the old glassware is selling cheaply. If you are lucky, the audience may be interested in the furniture and not the glassware. You may find it boxed and under tables. Perhaps you buy it for $20. a box, and then resell it for $100.!

Very low end estate auctions can have some neat finds. At a local "junky" auction, I picked up a group of old felt pendants for $1.00. I did not realize that one of these was an old "Karen and Richard Carpenter" pendant, circa 1960's, and was a fan club edition. It sold for more than $60.! The others sold for $25. My $1. investment turned into $85.. Not a bad profit.

CHAPTER 3: Where Do You Find "Good Junk"?

"Good Junk" can be found anywhere. Most pickers enjoy flea markets, garage sales, thrift shops and antique shops. Each venue has its own unique opportunities.

FLEA MARKETS:

Flea markets have a lot of merchandise from new to antique. Some vendors display their merchandise neatly in well-organized stalls. Others pile up their "junk" and set prices as they sell. Flea markets open early, often as early as six a.m. As the saying goes: "The early bird catches the worm." The best finds really are found early in the day as the vendors unpack their boxes. Flea market prices are usually negotiable. Always ask "What's your best price?" Be prepared to haggle price, but be careful not to insult the dealer. When an item is fairly priced, pay the price. It's important to make friends with the dealers. The more you buy from a dealer, the better the prices will be in the future.

Take a quick walk through the market at the end of your buying day. Some sellers will put goods out as the day wears on. Prices may even get better for you if it's a slow selling day. There are many great finds at flea markets. Look in boxes and under tables. A terrific example of this strategy was the Estate Filigree Bar Broach I found in a $2. costume jewelry box. It was 10 kt. gold with a small red stone. Its appraisal value was $225. The seller was unaware of its quality. Don't assume all sellers are experts or know the value of all of their merchandise.

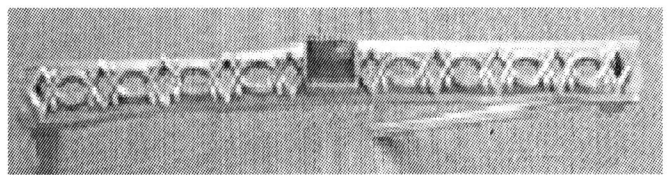

**A flea market find.
I paid $2.00. Valued at $225.00**

THRIFT SHOPS:

Thrift shops sell used merchandise. Their goods may come from a garage sale or an estate. Thrift shops are stores like the Salvation Army or Good Will. A thrift shop may also be operated by a private owner. They often carry glassware in addition to clothing and are generally very reasonably priced. Most of these shops have a better selection early in the week because families often clean out garages and attics on the weekend. Ask your shop owner when their staff puts out new inventory. Mark your calendar and plan on stopping in these shops weekly for some good buys.

GARAGE SALES:

Garage sales are time consuming. Watch for village-wide sales, where several families in a neighborhood set up a garage sale. You can find a lot of new and old things to sell. Often, the local Chamber of Commerce offices will have maps of these sales. Also, garage sales are usually listed in the classified section of your newspaper. Try looking in the paper midweek for the weekend sales. Plan your day, buy a street map and plot your travels to save time. Don't overlook baby items and kitchen things. You should always carry boxes and newspapers in your automobile to wrap your purchases. You will also need a quantity of small bills and change. Prices are negotiable.

Always ask for better prices.

In a city, it never hurts to scout out the sale the night before. Many people will be thrilled to sell early. Be polite and respect the ads. If the ad reads "no early birds," don't go ahead of time. Arrive very early the day of the sale and wait until the seller is ready to open.

ANTIQUE MALLS:
Antique malls are fabulous picking. You usually find a lot of interesting merchandise, nicely displayed and well labeled. It's a great place to find newer antique dealers who frequently underprice their goods. The larger the mall, the better the picking. Some of these malls will have more than a hundred dealers! Each dealer usually sets up an individual booth and fills their display cabinets with a variety of great items. You will find " Good Junk" to fine antiques. These shops almost always give dealer discounts. Introduce yourself as a dealer and inquire about a dealer discount. During slow seasons, discounts can be excellent. You can expect a 10% discount or more during the slow selling times. These shops also have store wide sale days. Expect to spend a few hours at the larger shops. Anticipate finding great items at fair prices!

Moss Rose spice set. Circa 1960's.
This piece had an old Woolworth store sticker on it.
I paid $27. at a Clarence Center, New York antique mall.
It sold on eBay for $251.76!

INDIVIDUAL "MOM AND POP" SHOPS:

No one can be an expert in everything. Keep in mind, not everyone is selling online. Owners of individually owned "Mom and Pop" shops may underestimate the selling appeal of items or just may not be knowledgeable in what's "hot" online. The advantage of smaller shops is that these owners can dramatically reduce prices if they choose to. They may heavily discount old inventory in order to recapture money for new inventory. Identify yourself as a fellow dealer and ask about their best price. You may be very surprised at the discounts they offer you. Don't let the sticker price stop you from inquiring.

Some shops are neat, and some are like a flea market.

1950s Chicken
Baby Feeder
I paid $8.00. It sold
on eBay for
$104.60
Found in a
Warrensburg, NY
"Mom and
Pop"Shop

"We accept cash, credit cards and good checks"

This statement was in the first auction ad I ever read. **"We accept cash, credit cards and good checks."** "Good check?" I repeated in my head, what's that? I asked everyone I knew; "What's a good check?" No one knew the answer. I thought perhaps they meant a cashier check but that didn't make any sense. How would I know how much I would spend? I really didn't want to charge my purchases. And cash.... who uses cash?

I arrived early the day of the auction. I previewed the goods. I knew just what I wanted to bid on. I brought my own chair. I had boxes and newspaper. I was sure no one would know I was a novice. I took my place in a very long line to sign in. Many people filed in behind me. After standing in line for fifteen minutes, it was my turn to sign in. I handed over my driver's license to the cashier, signed her sheet and received my number. Before walking away, I quietly asked her: "What's a good check?" She looked up and said "What?" She had a puzzled look on her face. I innocently asked her again: "What's a good check?" By that time, everyone in the building started laughing! Not one person had a straight face. The elderly lady smiled and said to me: "Honey, if you need to ask, then we don't need to worry about you. A good check, means it's not a **BAD** check!"

LOCAL AUCTIONS:
Local auctions are a great place to buy, but an even better place to learn! You can learn how to price your items. You will learn how much money area dealers are actually paying for goods. You will learn who the dealers are in your area. The only drawback is that you may sit for six hours to buy four items. It can be a rather slow process. I recommend you arrive early, preview items and then check in. Checking in at auctions can include showing some form of identification. I use my driver's license. Many auctioneers accept cash, credit cards or "good checks." Some do not accept credit cards. I suggest you bring cash to be safe. There will be a table set up, with a clerk. She will assign you a number card. This card should be used to bid. If you want to bid on an item, you will hold up your card. Be sure the auctioneer sees your card. Many people have lost their desired item thinking they were in the bidding, when it was actually the guy behind them that was seen! After the auction, you need to pay for your item. Auctioneers prefer you pay before you remove the merchandise. If you buy a heavy item, the

auction staff will usually help you load your car. If you buy an item too heavy to remove the day of the sale, you may be able to make arrangements to pick it up later. I always discuss these potential problems prior to the sale to avoid difficulties later.

Be aware that some auctioneers charge a "buyer's premium." This is an extra fee added to the final sale price. This may be as much as 10% of the sale. This fee can make an item less desirable to resell. Ask about buyer premiums before you bid.

Bring a pen, a blanket to cushion your items and a measuring tape with you. You will want to keep a list of your final bids to compare your list to the clerk's list when checking out. You will avoid any overcharges.

There are different types of local auctions. My favorite is the **estate auction**. Estate auctions are conducted after an individual has died. Families may have gone through the estate and removed a few obvious antiques but will usually leave a lot of wonderful "Good Junk." Some of my very best finds are from these auctions. You will find many box lots. Box lots are boxes filled with items the auctioneer may think is junk or he may believe these goods will not sell well for him. Sometimes it's a time factor. The estate may be very large and time will not allow for the small items to be sold individually. These boxes can make a " Good Junk" dealer a tidy profit. In order to buy the best box lots, you will need to arrive early. Usually the preview time is two hours prior to the sale. You will want to arrive at least an hour to ninety minutes ahead of the sale. Any items you may want to purchase need to be seen.

Items are sold "as is" and sales are final. Be aware. Never buy what you have not touched and inspected carefully. Box lots can hold wonderful treasures at low prices. Anything in the box lot you don't want can be given to a garage sale dealer {you will see many of them in the audience}, or plan a yearly garage sale of your own to sell your unwanted items. Box lots often are auctioned off last, so be prepared to spend the day.

Another type of auction that can hold some good buys is a **consignment auction**. These auctions usually are items that individuals have given to the auctioneer to auction for them. Dealers may offer items for an auction during slow selling times or to liquidate old inventory. These auctions can include "Good Junk" mixed in with higher end antiques. I, personally, do not enjoy these as much as an estate auction. You can find the occasional good buy but that does not happen very often.

Another auction type I do enjoy is the auctioning off of a **store's contents**. These are great if it's an antique and collectibles shop. The small items are often sold in box lots and you can buy a quantity of similar items. When buying items in quantity, prices can be very reasonable.

Auction prices can get out of control due to auction fever! Individuals will keep on bidding, even after a price is out of line. Decide what you want to pay for an item and do not second guess yourself. You will be bidding against individual bidders as well as dealers. Collectors will pay book price or even more at times.

Bring along a comfortable folding chair and try attending on bad weather days. Fewer people attend on rainy, cold days and that means less competition on your bids. One of the best buys I ever made was on a sunny day that unexpectedly turned wet and cold. The auctioneer did not have a tent. The auction was more than seventy miles from my home. I always travel with a coat and umbrella in my trunk. The sale was full of fine antiques. The audience was sparse to begin with because this was a very rural location. I doubt that we started with more than fifty buyers. When the wind starting blowing and rain poured down, many people left. Even though we had only about twenty bidders, the auctioneer decided to continue. He sold many items from inside the house. We sat in the rain, as he described the items. Luckily, I had previewed the items carefully before the auction. I walked away with a late 1860's fainting couch for $300. It was valued at $1200. At any other auction I would not have been able to buy this so inexpensively.

Auctions are fun and can be profitable. Be prepared to invest some time. Always arrive prepared. Bring boxes and paper to wrap your items. Have a great time but know when to back off on your bidding.

FAMILY AND FRIENDS:
Often co-workers, family or friends will offer to sell you their treasures. Many people don't like having garage sales. This can be tricky. What if an item you bought from your Aunt sells **REALLY** well and you paid very little for it? Will you feel guilty or will she be upset? I personally avoid buying from family and friends whenever possible. There is too much room for personal problems.

Wonderful 1940's green Depression glass slipper. This little green slipper holds two little perfume bottles. The bottom of the slipper is marked "Japan". It was purchased in Reno, Nevada for $35.

ONLINE AUCTIONS:

Try buying from online auctions during slow selling seasons ie: holiday weeks and summer time. Dealers are setting opening bids low and there are fewer buyers. It's a really good combination to buy inexpensively and sell well, later. Just keep in mind, you are also paying for shipping, which can get costly. Ask about the shipping costs in advance to avoid costly surprises.

ESTATES:

Buying a complete household estate can be a very profitable adventure. Some dealers will advertise to buy a complete estate. These households become available when a family needs to dispose of an individual's home following his death or placement in a nursing home. After the family removes the obvious better pieces, there will almost always be some " Good Junk" left to choose from. Families will often recognize an antique piece or good glass but will under estimate the value of Pyrex, old toys and smaller items such as perfume bottles. They may not want to have a garage sale. Many families just are too busy to conduct the sales. Some families may just want the sale to be over. They will not want the hassle of selling it themselves.

Pricing these households can be tricky. Personally I have never purchased an estate but I have been lucky enough to see others do it. You must take a good look at the larger items and place a resale value on them. Secondly you must consider the quality and condition of the "Good Junk." Are there many nice pieces of old kitchenware, glass, lacy linens, toys and vintage holiday items? Do you see newer items that may sell well? This really is an area that requires experience and a bit of luck. The major obstacle to buying a complete household is where to store the items after the purchase. You will also need to remove it all from the home. That involves a truck and man power. All of these require the possibility of incurring a cash output. This may be a better option for an industrious family. If you have the room to store the merchandise and the manpower to do this, I can see this option as a nice alternative to the weekly shopping trips. A full household could take you weeks, if not months to sell off. There is no doubt you will find lots of hidden treasures.

ESTATE TAG SALES:

Some families hire antique dealers to hold a public sale of their loved one's household. The sale is held in the house. Items are priced and tagged. They will limit how many buyers are allowed in the house at a one time. As buyers leave, new ones are allowed in. Dealers will arrive very early and wait in line. There are many variations on this type of sale. Some sales give you a number and you pull the price tag from an item and put in on your number sheet. When you are finished, a clerk will retrieve your items. Some sellers allow you to pick up your items as you find them. Ask questions in advance. These sales can offer good buys to "Good Junk" dealers. A lot of lower priced items will be overlooked by the local antique dealers. This is a great way to try "guesses." An item you pay $1. for, could sell on eBay for $20. or more. I often arrive late in the day. Prices get reduced toward the end of the sale. Families do not want junk to deal with after the sale.

GARBAGE /TRASH DAY:

Yes, garbage picking can be profitable. Don't overlook searching for things on trash day. Super finds are out there. I know a gentleman who does it regularly and then takes the items to his local auctioneer. He makes a lot of money selling old furniture, lawn items and used wood doors. He finds them on trash day. Try looking in better neighborhoods, or older sections of town. I can remember being horrified as a teenager seeing an old man picking through our basement throw-a-ways. Now I find me strangely attracted to the piles near the road!

There **IS** money in " Good Junk", but first learn what is good! Never miss an opportunity to buy. Stop at antique shops or flea markets on road trips. Use these shopping stops as your rest stop. Plan a visit to a flea market early on your vacation day, even as your mate sleeps. A brief stop on a trip can produce enough income from good buys to offset your vacation expenses. You also may be able to write off some of the traveling expenses as business expenses.

CHAPTER 4: Where Do You Sell Your "Good Junk"?

You will sell your merchandise in the same places you buy it! You will sell "Good Junk" in flea markets, antique malls, thrift shops and garage sales. Why? Because our best customers are often other dealers. This will also apply to selling online. Certainly there are collectors out there, but many of them also deal in "Good Junk" or fine antiques. Here is a list of my favorite places to sell. These are not all of your choices, but some of the best!

ONLINE AUCTIONS:
There are many online auction sites to choose from. My favorites are eBay and Yahoo. I've tried a few others but I find these two to produce the best results for me. eBay has a huge customer base. Buyers are from around the world. I've sold to customers in Japan, Germany, France, Australia, England, the Netherlands and nearly all 50 United States. eBay is easy to use, has a great bulk auction listing tool and usually produces a good price for your product. You can sell almost anything on eBay. They have a system in place to discourage non-paying bidders. It is very effective. eBay demands a better quality seller and buyer.

Yahoo has some great advantages. It is inexpensive and easy to navigate. Picture quality is great. They allow multiple free pictures with each item. It's a great place to try selling items you paid a little too much for. Listing fees are quite inexpensive. Some listing fees are as low as five cents! On this site you can afford to have an item not sell. Auction sites allow relisting of items that did not sell, often without a second fee if your item sells the second time around. It is easy to make money in as little as ten days. Auctions are fast, easy and fun. There are a few different auction formats.

Auction formats include the following:

Straight auctions:
The seller sets a minimum bid and the bidders begin bidding. The follow-up bids increase until the end of the auction. The auctions will last three, five, seven or ten days. Bid increments are set by the site. This is the type of auction where sellers generally sell one-of-a kind items.

Dutch auctions:
To put this in simple terms, a seller has a quantity of the same or similar items for sale. He sets an opening bid and the quantity he has to sell. The ending price is the lowest price achieved at the end of the auction. This may be a bit confusing. I suggest you check each auction site to determine their policy regarding "Dutch" auctions.

Reserve auctions:
This is an auction where the seller has set the minimum price he will accept for an item. The reserve price is not listed in the description. Some sellers will reveal the reserve price if you ask. As a seller you can determine your policy regarding discussing the reserve with potential buyers. Some auction sites charge a hefty fee if a seller uses the option of reserving an auction. Most buyers really dislike reserve auctions. I find bidding is less active when I use this feature.

ONLINE WEB STORES:

There are many online Web Stores. Web stores are often a group of individual dealers gathered together to sell on one Internet site. Each shop owner has his/her own business heading. You name your shop. You can visualize this by thinking of a local mall. A mall has one large building with many stores within it. Each store has an owner. Each store provides its own merchandise.

An example of this online is **Cyberattic.com**, which can be found at **http://www.cyberattic.com**. **Cyberattic** is my favorite Internet Web store site. It is a large site with many different shops. It is incredibly easy to use. Their webmaster sets up your store front. You provide him/her with the information about your business. You should include your shop's name, your line of merchandise, and your shipping policies. After your store is set up, you will be provided with an online location to start listing your items. In this area, you will include an item description, a price and a picture. You have total control of listing your items. Your customers will deal directly with you. There is no bidding. Customers will pay the price you have listed in your ad. They also pay a shipping fee based on where they live. I use the United States Postal Service to mail their items after I receive payment. My **Cyberattic** customers are from all around the world. Sales are private, just between you and your customer. You can decide what payments you will accept. I like to accept money orders, checks and many of the online third party payment services like PayPal. Your e-mail address is your contact address. This is perhaps the least expensive web store selling site online for selling good junk. Pictures are of a very good quality. You can get top dollar for your merchandise. **Cyberattic** is a site to sell antiques, collectibles and " Good Junk." New items are best sold elsewhere. Fees are paid on a yearly basis. There are currently NO commission fees.

This little cut glass butter pat dish was found at a garage sale in Ontario, Canada. It has a beautiful opalescent quality. The edges are very crisp and cut. I paid $.70 for this piece. It sold on eBay for $20.00.

FLEA MARKETS:

Flea market stalls are usually rented by the day or weekend. In some areas they are in heated or air-conditioned buildings that remain open all week. You can sell almost anything from fine antiques to real junk. Generally you need to stay in your booth and sell your own goods.

GARAGE SALES:

Garage sales are a nice, easy way to sell your goods from your own home. You will need to check on local restrictions. Your items need to be priced clearly. Do not expect to sell fine collectibles and antiques. You will need to expect to negotiate your prices. Buyers will almost always ask you to accept less money.

MULTI-DEALER SHOPS:

Multi-dealer shops are a wonderful way to sell better merchandise. These shops will have many dealers in the same building. You can choose a booth or a display cabinet. These shops have a clerk. You do not need to be there to sell. You should expect to pay higher fees when selling in this type of shop. Prices need to be clearly marked. Price tags need to be labeled with a dealer number, item number and a price. Price tags can be purchased from a local business supply store or from the shop owner. Remember to always attach the price tags in a manner that will not damage the item. I affix tags directly on unpainted glass or pottery. Paper items should have a tag placed on a separate piece of paper and slipped into the item. Never attach a sticky tag to paper goods. Damage to the book cover, album cover or a box can greatly reduce your selling price. Shops will vary as to rules regarding price tag types. Contracts are signed. The contract usually obligates you to six months of paying their monthly fees.

BACKYARD SHOPS:

Backyard shops are really another great option to sell your goods. The disadvantage is you need to be home to sell. Due to the need to be in your shop, it is much tougher to find time to shop for inventory. Prices usually are expected to be less expensive than in a "real" shop. This type of selling is a bit more challenging, but fun. You can open at your convenience or adhere to regular hours.

ANTIQUE SHOWS:

Another selling option is selling at antique shows. Most cities and many smaller towns have a yearly antique show and sale. These shows can be fine antiques or flea market style events. Some are huge. Others may be quite small. You can buy your " Good Junk" all year and sell in these shows. Fine antique shows may be juried. Juried shows will have standards. You may have to be accepted into these shows by an individual or a committee. Standards or criteria can be stiff. It can be based on concrete criteria such as the type of goods you sell or abstract criteria. Abstract criteria may be as vague as you meeting the show's exhibit theme.

Many shows are not difficult to be accepted into. If you can pay their fee, you will be included. Fees can vary greatly from show to show. It can be quite costly but I have found that dealers can ask top dollar for their items.

Customers will ask for your best price. Antique shows usually are open on Friday, Saturday and Sunday. There are outdoor shows in the spring, summer and fall. Winter antique shows are generally held inside large buildings. Many shows will require that you operate a legitimate business. You may need to have a tax exempt number. You may be required to collect sales tax. These details need to be investigated in advance. Outdoor shows may require that you supply your own display tables and a canopy to protect you from the weather. Indoor shows usually provide a few basics. Additional display shelving is a plus. In order to really understand these events, I suggest you visit a few to get the feel of them. My personal favorite is the show in Brimfield, Massachusetts. The Brimfield Show operates three times a year during May, July and September and is open for a six-day period beginning on a Tuesday and ending on a Sunday. Some field operators open all six days while others choose to open for just a few days during this period. To sign up you need to decide what shows you want to be in and contact the individual owner. Each field has its own separate owner. The Brimfield web site has all the information you will need, **http://www.brimfield.com**. There are as many as five thousand dealers in this show. It is a fun place to buy or sell.

OTHER OPTIONS:
Because of the length of this book, it is not possible to list all the selling arenas available to you. In fairness I must admit there are many others. I have listed my favorite sites and my personal preferences for selling. I strongly suggest you try an online search to discover all your options. Your choices may be very different from mine.

ADVERTISING:
Advertising of your selling locations is another important aspect of your business. Potential customers need to know where to find your goods. I use the "signature" area on my e-mail to list my web store link and my auction sites. I include my identifying name for each site. Also try using business cards that list your selling locations. Always hand your business cards out to potential customers. You should never miss the opportunity to discuss your online business and promote your sites. It is up to you to sell your business and to promote your selling locations.

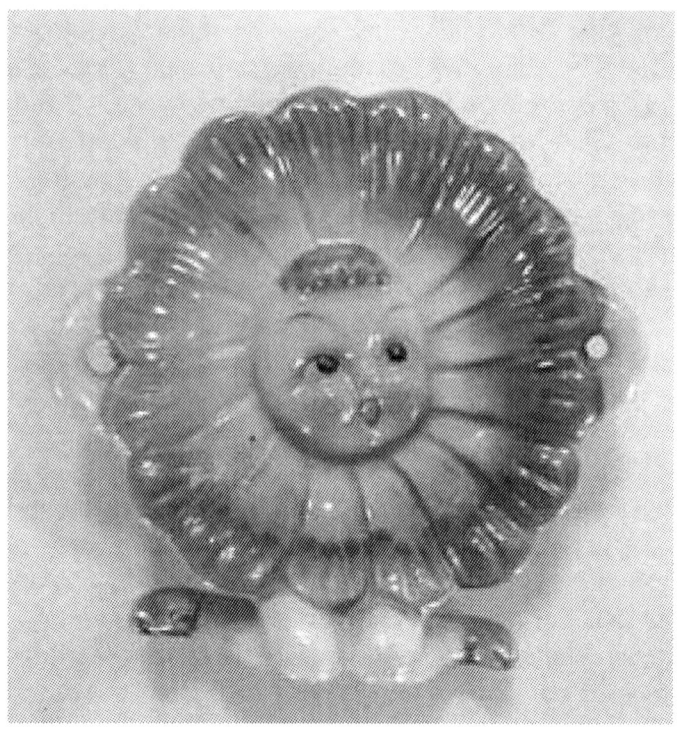

This lovely, colorful tea bag holder was found at a local thrift shop. She has a wonderful face. This piece was unmarked. I paid $1.00 for her. She sold for $15.50 on eBay.

CHAPTER 5: How Do You Determine a Price For Your "Good Junk"?

Selling online requires a few learned skills. Learning how to set a price is very important. To maximize your profit you need a well worded, detailed description of your item, excellent closeup pictures and some knowledge of your merchandise. Categorizing on an online auction site can be tricky, but by doing a little advance research, you can quickly learn how to best utilize the categories. Research your item by seeing what category other dealers have already listed a similar item in. You will learn that if you have found one of these items, someone else has already sold one.

I personally like to try an eBay "completed item" search. An eBay "completed item" search is easy to do. After logging onto the eBay site, you will find a "search" button on the top of the page. You will click on the "search" button. This will direct you to the search area. You will see many options. At this time you will choose "completed items" search. Click on the "completed items" search button. On the next page you will type in what you are looking for. It is a very effective tool. You probably will find items like yours. They will include the selling price and category it was sold in. You can try selling your item in that category. If you do not find an item like yours, you will need to decide what category it would best fit in. Sometimes it's a guess. Once the category is decided, you are ready to list your item.

Pricing depends on where you will be selling your product. When selling on an online auction site, I set my price at the least amount I can afford to accept for the item. That is determined by what I paid for it and my estimated selling cost. That is my starting point. Other sellers use a collector's guide book to estimate a selling price. If I'm selling in a local shop, I use a price closer to the book price and what fellow dealers are charging for a similar item in my area. Go window shopping to learn current product trends and pricing. Frequenting local shops and flea markets will increase your general knowledge of "Good Junk" and pricing. To be successful selling in a shop, you need to be competitively priced.

Online web store sellers usually set a price on items close to the book price. Collectors' guide books are found in all major retail book stores and libraries. You can buy them new or used. I like them for identification and also for pricing. They can be costly but they do become a part of your research library. Book prices are really just estimates of selling prices. They are meant to determine price on perfect pieces. Defects or chips will greatly decrease your item's value. If I have overpaid for the item or the item is harder to find, I may set a higher price.

Online Collector clubs are another great research area. Try doing a general online search via a web engine like Yahoo. When on the web engine search page, you will type in the item you want to research. If you are trying to price a piece of Fenton glass, type in "Fenton." A number of pages will be available to you. You will need to preview them and find a club site or the manufacturer's home page. Once you find these clubs, you will usually find prices, rare item listings and some general merchandise information.

The bottom line is to not lose money selling your item

and to make as much as you can. Keep in mind, to make money you need to spend money. You will need to sell your inventory to purchase new inventory. Experience will be your best teacher. If you lose money on an item today, you will pay less for it next time or you will avoid it all together.

CHAPTER 6: How Do You Get Organized?

This is **THE** most important chapter in this book! You can have great merchandise, a perfect description, a good price, and you can still remain so "unorganized" that you never get it to market! You must have good basic organizational skills. Plan a weekly shopping day or two. Consider it a work day. Take yourself seriously or others won't. Learn the best days to go to flea markets or garage sales in your area. Keep a calender of the village-wide sale days. I find that weekend mornings are usually best for these activities. Plan to spend as many as four hours on Saturday and Sunday picking "Good Junk".

If you decide to sell in an online Web Store, you need to keep a list of items you plan to always sell in your shop. Buy these items weekly. Do not frantically shop after you have a customer's order for an item. Anticipate your customers' needs. Time wasted looking for an item is lost income. Remember... time <u>IS</u> money.

A well-organized room in your house is essential. Setting up an area in your home where you can add shelving, pack your items and store your inventory is critical. A separate room helps you remain organized. I like a room large enough to keep inventory separate from the items that are waiting to be shipped. Each wall can be shelved to hold items at different stages of the transaction. The better you are organized, the more time you have to buy and sell. **More time to sell equals more income!**

Record keeping may seem a bit boring, but in the long run it'll save you time and help you avoid frustration. It's my least favorite part of the "Good Junk" business. Keep your record keeping simple in the beginning. Hand written records are just as valuable as computer generated ones, especially if your computer expertise is limited. Keeping separate notebooks is the easiest way to keep well organized.

I keep a notebook for **inventory**. For each item I include the date the item was purchased, the item's name and the price I paid for it. Also, I include an assigned item number and a column for the selling price and date of sale.

You will also need a way of tracking your **income**. You should include columns for the date and amount of money that you take in. You will also need to keep track of any items you keep for personal use. Items kept for personal use are considered income to you.

Mileage traveled to purchase your goods (and return mileage) must be logged. I keep a little notebook over the sun-visor in my car. This log sheet is necessary because work related mileage is tax-deductible, but you need to keep a record of the date and the actual mileage that you travel to purchase your goods.

You will also need a notebook to keep track of **business expenses**. This notebook should include everything you spend on your business. Don't forget to include paper goods and supplies for your office or shipping material that you buy, computer items, road tolls and anything else you think may be considered a business expense. You can reevaluate these expenses at tax time.

An **item location** notebook is a book that lists where I'm selling an item. I have an eBay and a Cyberattic.com notebook. In these I list the item, assign an inventory number and sale price. The eBay book has an area to check off if the customer has contacted me after winning the bid.

I prefer using notebooks (the "old fashioned way"), but you can also use a small business software program on a computer - - just be sure you have a back-up disk in case your system crashes or you get a virus! It may sound complicated, but once you find a "system" that works for you, it will really make running your business a lot easier.

After receiving my customer's shipping information, I input that into an invoice form that I have on my computer. Your invoice should clearly indicate your customer's shipping address and the item he's buying. Write the selling price and shipping cost on this paper and keep it with the item. This saves you time spent searching for lost addresses. It also helps you avoid shipping a product to the wrong customer! This is a mistake we have all made, which is time consuming and can be costly. Items with an invoice (or packing slip) can be more easily identified for shipping.

If you are using an online auction, contact your customer quickly after an auction closes. Use standardized e-mail responses whenever possible (its quick and it saves you money on postage). More will be discussed on this subject later in the book (Chapter 11), including examples of useful e-mail.

SAMPLE FORMS

Inventory: List the date you purchased your item, where it was purchased, the items name and how much you paid for it. A column is needed to list the actual selling price. A paper notebook or a computer software program like "C.A.D." by Tinkerware L.L.C., which can be found at **www.tinkerware.com**, can be used to list inventory. If interested, go to their web site and take a tour of their program. If you prefer the handwritten method, try the following sample form.

Date	Item/Item #	Price Paid	Selling Price	Date Sold

Income: All monies you receive from your sales need to be accounted for. You can use a notebook or computer software program like Microsoft "Money", **http://www.microsoft.com**, to record your income and business expenses. If interested, this program can be purchased at a computer software store or online. You can preview it at the Microsoft web site listed above. They have a list of all their products on their web site.

Date	Income	Comments

Selling Location Book: This book keeps track of where you are selling an item. It lists the item, an assigned inventory number, the price paid for it and the selling price.

Item/Item #	Where selling item	Price Paid	Selling Price

Business expenses: Business expenses are almost anything you use in your business. They can include your office supplies, computer, notebooks, and more. You will be able to offset a portion of your income with these expenses.

Date	Business Expense	Where Incurred	Comments

Mileage: Keeping a log of the mileage you travel to buy your goods is another business expense. These miles can add up to quite a few dollars, and often can be deducted from your taxable income at the end of the year.

Date	Destination	Mileage

Payments to you: Keep another notebook to keep track of what monies you have paid yourself and any inventory items that you keep for your personal use. If you are tax exempt, you will need to pay the sales tax on items you keep or give as gifts.

Date	Item	Price paid

Sales tax: If you decide to set up your business to collect sales tax in your state, you need accurate records of all sales tax money you collect. There are advantages in doing so. When you buy inventory purchases, you will not pay sales tax to other dealers. You become sales tax exempt. I advise attending a local evening program that discusses setting up a small business in your state. These are often offered at local community colleges. You will learn the advantages and disadvantages of collecting sales taxes and reporting them to local governments.

Date	Items sale price	Sales tax collected

When you sell an item for someone else and receive a **commission**, you need to keep accurate records. You will not want to pay income tax on the complete sale. Keeping track of the fees charged to sell the item is important. You will charge your client the fees plus your commission.

Date	Item	Where sold	Amount Paid	Fees Paid	Com-mis-sion	Total due

Other organizational tips will follow in Chapter 11, on "Good Customer Service."

CHAPTER 7: What Equipment Do You Need to Sell "Good Junk"?

Your equipment needs will vary. It depends on how sophisticated you want to get. It also depends on where you want to sell. I will deal with your online needs here. This is the area most people become nervous about. Don't get scared. I will take you through the process slowly and gently. Selling on the Internet will require the following equipment:

A COMPUTER:
A computer can be expensive, but....you do not need a high priced, fast computer. Try finding a used or free one (yes.... I said "free"!) I started with a hand-me-down computer from my daughter. She was upgrading to a newer, faster (more expensive) model and had no use for the "old" one anymore. It was slow but it worked well. I had never touched a computer before, and had NO computer knowledge at all. But, I had the desire to sell online and the determination to learn. If you can afford to invest in a new computer, you will find most department discount stores have entry level computers at reasonable prices. If you don't want to buy a new one, then ask your friends if they are upgrading, check the classified ads in your local newspaper for used computers, and ask someone that you know who works in an office what they do with their "old" computers.

INTERNET PROVIDERS:
After getting your computer and setting it up, the next decision you need to make is how you are going to

connect to the Internet. There are a few different ways to this. Each option has a different monthly cost.

The most common is probably **dial-up**. One well-known example of a dial-up Internet provider is AOL. (America On Line). Dial-up Internet provider fees usually cost from $9.95 to $25.00 a month. You will need a modem, which most computers have. A modem allows your computer to connect to the Internet via your telephone line. This connection can be slower than other options, and its speed will depend on your local telephone service. You can buy this service by looking in your local telephone book under Internet services. Be careful to check if the dial-up number is a local number in your area or you may incur long distance telephone charges. There are many local Internet servers.

Although this is the cheapest method of going online, there are two disadvantages. When you are online, the telephone line to your telephone is busy so you cannot use your telephone for incoming or outgoing calls. And second, when someone is using the telephone in the house, you cannot go online to conduct business. This may not be a good system for large families.

Another option is a broadband Internet provider. These are referred to as **DSL**. These are incredibly fast, but can be pricy at approximately $39.95 a month. But, this service will save you time (and some aggravation) in conducting business online. These services may not be available in all areas. You can find information regarding the availability of these services in your area by looking in your local telephone book. They will be listed under Internet in most directories. Although this method is more expensive, it is a better method (faster) and about the same price as paying for two phone lines into your house (one for the family to use and one for your business).

A third service is called **Web TV.** This service actually uses your television set, and you use a keyboard to navigate the Internet via your television. You need to buy a receiver. These currently are selling for $99.00. In addition, you will pay a monthly fee of approximately $9.99. It's described as "the easy and affordable alternative for those just starting out on the Internet." It's easy to set up and easy to use. You just hook it up to a television and a phone line and register for the monthly service. Be careful that the connection is a local telephone number for you or you may incur long distance charges from your telephone company. As with all options, consider all the fees involved.

All these connections will allow you to conduct business online. You must decide how much money you want to spend monthly. I must admit I still use the dial-up method. It's inexpensive and fast enough for me!

CALLWAVE:
Callwave is an online telephone answering service. It works like an answering machine. When you are online and someone calls you, they will get a prerecorded message. It will request that they leave you a message. You will hear the message over your computer. It can include a caller ID feature. This service is quite inexpensive and can be billed to your telephone company. Payments can be monthly or yearly. I currently pay less than $35.00 a year including the caller ID feature. This is a terrific savings when you consider the cost of a second telephone line in your home, **http://www.callwave.com**.

DIGITAL CAMERA:

Pictures of your merchandise are necessary to sell your item. Keep in mind, your customer cannot touch or feel this item. A customer needs to at least see it. I suggest a digital camera. These cameras takes pictures that are stored on a small floppy disc card. The pictures are then moved to your computer via a cable. Each camera comes with detailed instructions regarding this process. Pictures can be edited for size and quality. Cameras generally come with the software program to accomplish this. It may sound difficult but it really is not.

You need to find a digital camera with a macro feature. This allows for closeups. Closeup pictures are important to show details and defects. Digital cameras can cost as little as $50.00. They can be purchased in discount department stores, drugstores and camera shops.

A PRINTER:

A printer is very handy in your business. I like to copy the e-mail that includes my customer's shipping address. I keep this paper with the merchandise until I ship it. When shipping time comes, I cut out the shipping information and tape it to the box. This saves time and helps me avoid errors in mailing addresses. Printers can be very inexpensive. A used one .. or free one... would be just fine. I see them in garage sales frequently. Expect to pay as little as $20.00 for a used one. New printers can cost $80.00 or more in discount stores. Price shop for a great deal.

SCALES:

You will need a scale that weighs ounces and one that can weigh up to 20 pounds. Pre-weighing your items and checking the shipping costs online can save you a lot of time. You will have packages ready to go in a hurry.

Scales are easy to find and need not be expensive. Buy used scales if you can.

NOTEBOOKS, ETC.:

Notebooks can be purchased at a dollar store. These can be any style you like. I use large notebooks with a metal spiral binding for almost all my office needs. Buy half a dozen notebooks to start. Don't forget to buy pens, pencils, stapler, scotch tape, packing tape, and any other office material you may need. (You can usually get a lot of your office supplies at a dollar store, too).

BUSINESS CARDS:

Business cards can be purchased online. These sites often have special deals. You can frequently buy 200 custom-made cards for the shipping cost only! I personally use VistaPrint, **http://www.vistaprint.com**. It is an easy to navigate web site. They have many great card designs. Business cards are handy to leave with shop owners or to give to potential customers. They are a great way to advertise your business. When designing your business cards, include your selling sites and your e-mail address on your cards. You can order business cards from a stationery or business supply store like Staples.

There is a lot of luxury equipment you can buy. These items can include inventory software and a photo reader for your camera. But, you do not **NEED** to invest a lot of money. Start small and just buy the equipment and supplies that you **REALLY** need to start with. Add equipment that saves you time or adds to the quality of your work environment once you get your business up, running and profitable.

CHAPTER 8: What Does it Cost to Sell Your "Good Junk"?

The cost of doing business really depends on where you decide to sell your merchandise. One thing is for sure -- there are fees and/or commissions to be paid. I have included many general fees you may encounter. Specific fees related to selling may vary in your local area. Online fees can change fairly frequently.

ONLINE AUCTIONS:
Listing fees: A listing fee is a fee charged to list an item for sale on an auction site. It is based on the opening bid of your item. They can range from a few cents to a few dollars. These are usually non refundable if your item does not sell. Some sites allow you to relist an item, and if it sells on the second try, you do not pay a second fee.

Final value fees: Final value fees are fees paid on the total price your customer pays for the item. If it sells for $25., you pay a percentage of the selling price as a fee. These fees can run from a few cents to a few dollars. They vary again depending on which auction site you use.

Other fees: Other fees can include a small fee to add luxuries within the auction site. Some of these features include the following:

Setting a **Reserve** on your item {the lowest amount of money you will accept for it}, will cost you a fee. These fees can be a bit pricy. The Insertion Fee is based on the reserve price of the item you list for sale. You will also be charged a Reserve Price Auction Fee, which is also based upon the reserve price. If your item sells, the Reserve Price Auction Fee is refunded to your account. Use the reserve feature carefully. These fees add up very quickly. Customers are not fond of reserved items. You may not receive as many bids as you would have expected. A reserve can be a good idea if you overpaid for the item or if you know it's value and cannot take less than the book price.

Auctions that run more than seven days will incur a small fee. This usually occurs if you want your auction to run **ten days**, instead of the usual three, five or seven days. This is a very minor expense. Ten day auctions are useful during your vacation times. You can keep auctions running while you are away from your computer.

The " **Buy -It-Now**" feature has a fee. This feature allows you to set a price that you will accept any time during the auction. When a customer chooses this feature, the auction ends immediately.

Listing an item in **more than one category** will cost you double the usual listing fee. This is more costly. It can be very useful for items that are more expensive and need greater customer exposure.

A little picture that appears near your items heading can be very useful. They are called **gallery** pictures. Many auction sites have this feature that allows customers to shop for items by picture only. If the customer likes the picture, she/he can click on the picture to get a full description of the item. Each site charges a different fee for this special feature. The fee is worth the cost to you. Customers really like to see a picture before going into the full listing. It saves them time when looking for an item.

Adding **Bold** print to your listing heading can really add emphasis to your item. There is a fee for this feature.

The **Featured** item feature is very pricy. Your merchandise will be shown prominently in the Featured Items section of its category list. It will also appear in the regular, non-featured item list. It can be very useful for the high-priced items.

There are other special features. I advise looking at the features offered on your chosen auction site. You will need to review the fees charged to avoid excessive selling expenses.

Many of these services can maximize your sale potential. Choose these carefully because these fees can add up quickly and each fee takes away from your profits.

WEB STORES:
Web store fees are often charged on a yearly basis. Some stores also charge a commission on each sale. These fees can be approximately 10% of a sale. Fees vary greatly from store front to store front. My favorite storefront site is **http:\\www. Cyberattic.com** and they charge a yearly fee. As of this writing date, it is $50. for up to 500 ads. Each ad may include five pictures. If you want the site to host your pictures, you may purchase a Premium membership at an additional annual fee of $60. yearly. Your total cost is $110. a year for 500 listings. They do not charge any other fees. This service is very reasonable. More information on this site is in Chapter 4.

GARAGE SALES:

Garage sales are a nice easy way to dispose of unsold inventory. The fees depend on your local paper. Newspaper ads should cost less than $15.. Local "Pennysaver" ads are even less expensive. A good garage sale ad should include the date and hours of your sale. Your address needs to be clear. If you are difficult to find, include some physical details. I advise giving mileage from a popular intersection to your home. In your ad, always list a few of your better items for sale. If it's to be held indoors be sure to include that information. A rain date is a good idea if you are selling outdoors.

FLEA MARKETS:

Flea markets usually charge a daily or a weekend fee based on table size. Some flea markets are held indoors. Flea markets are often open seven days a week. They often charge a monthly stall fee. In addition, some markets have a small commission fee based on sale prices. These markets have a clerk and you do not need to be in your booth all day.

MULTI-DEALER SHOPS OR ANTIQUE MALLS:

Antique malls and multi-dealer shops usually charge a monthly fee and a commission based on your total sales. They frequently require a selling contract. Some shops also have store wide mandatory sale days. They will discount all merchandise in a shop by a predetermined percentage. Ask the owner what their policies are in advance of signing a contract. One large advantage is these shops have clerks. You are not required to remain in your booth. Your customer's money is collected for you. You will receive a monthly check minus your applicable fees.

MISCELLANEOUS FEES:

PayPal is an easy-to-use site. It is an online third party payment service that allows customers to pay you by credit card or electronic check. They charge the seller a small fee, very much like a shop owner pays to accept credit cards in his store, **http://www.paypal.com.**

Yahoo PayDirect by HSBC bank, is Yahoo auction sites customer payment service that allows customers to pay you by credit card for Yahoo auction and web store purchases. The seller is charged a fee for this service, **http://paydirect.yahoo.com.**

Bidpay {Western Union} is an online third party payment service that allows customers to pay you by credit card or money order. The customer is charged a fee. The money order is mailed to the seller by BidPay, **http:///www.bidpay.com**.

There are other online third party payment services that allow customers to pay you by credit card, money order or check. Most of these third party companies charge the seller a small fee. They are very similar to the fees a store owner incurs when accepting credit cards. Fees vary depending on which third party company you use.

I personally accept payments from most of them. In my opinion, these fees are a necessary cost of doing business. They are well worth the charges and definitely boost your sales. Customers like instant purchasing. Items are paid for quickly and you can ship very quickly. To find others, try a search on a search engine like Yahoo. Type in "online payments" and you will be surprised how many there are.

Image hosting:
If selling online, you need a picture {image} of your item to sell it. You can purchase space from an image hosting site. Sales will increase. The quality of pictures is important and does vary by hosting site. Most image hosting sites charge a fee. You can buy a hosting package of images only or a full selling package. Some sites include auction listing devices and some really neat extra selling services. There are some free sites. I find many of these sites complicated and not user friendly.

In the beginning, I encourage computer novices to take the easiest route. Use the picture services offered by the auction site. They are very simple to use. The quality of images does vary from auction site to auction site. After you get comfortable with selling online, investigate your other options. If you are already computer literate, try my favorite image hosting site, **http://www.andale.com**. It's very user friendly, fees are reasonable and the quality of pictures is great. Andale is worth a look. They have a terrific site for selling online. In fairness, I must add there are many image hosting sites. Try a few and decide which one you like best.

Bank Fees:
 Banking fees are probably unavoidable if you decide to accept personal checks. You will want a checking account. You will need one if you use third party payment services like PayPal. These services will deposit your customers' money into your account. It is also nice to have checks for inventory purchases. Keep in mind that many banks require a bank account to cash checks. You can set up a business checking or a personal checking account. Fees vary on these types of accounts. Business checking accounts accept checks with your business name

on them. In my experience you cannot cash a check with your business name on it, if you use a personal checking account only. You need to decide how your customers' checks will be made out to you, as a business or in your name. I suggest discussing both options with your bank. Shop around to find a bank that charges reasonable monthly or per check fees.

CHAPTER 9: How Do You Get Your Item to Your Customer?

Selling online adds a new dimension to your business. Shipping! You need to wrap your item, box it and ship it. Packaging and shipping is a very important step in your online business. Your customer has just paid you $40. to buy a memory, the same Pyrex range top coffee pot her grandmother used. The last thing either of you wants to happen is a broken item. It will greatly disappoint your customer and it will cost you time to help her process her postal insurance claim. To avoid these problems you need excellent packing materials and good packing skills. Shipping supplies can be expensive but I have found many ways to cut the costs. Recycling can help!

Here are some tips:

U.S. POSTAL SERVICE:
U.S. Priority Mail service shipping supplies are free through the U.S. Postal Service. They will supply you with boxes, priority tape, and labels. In addition to that, they will deliver them to your home. You can easily order them online. This is a great service. It is free! They also have a section on how to wrap and package your goods for shipping. It includes many helpful hints, **http://www.usps.com**.

BOXES:
Plain brown boxes can be obtained from your workplace, local stores, gift shops and from friends and co-workers. These are needed for nonpriority shipping. You may not

use the free boxes from the U.S. Postal Service for shipping any other way than Priority. Stock up on these plain boxes ahead of time. Keep a stock of them in various sizes. Use these boxes for U.S. mail first class and parcel post shipments. They also may be needed for other shipping services. You must always check your shipping services' policies regarding boxes.

PACKING PEANUTS:
Packing peanuts are really good cushioning material. It is tougher to find this product free but well worth the search. Ask your local gift shops, mall stores and family and friends to keep these for you. Customers appreciate the professional packing materials, and your items arrive safer.

SHREDDED PAPER:
Shredded paper is not generally the best cushioning material but it can be effective for less delicate items. You can easily find shredded paper in business offices. They will be happy to share it with you. All your junk mail is potential shipping material, if you use a paper shredder at home!

PADDED ENVELOPES/TAPE:
You can easily find shipping materials from office supply stores and online but it can be very costly. The more you pay for shipping supplies the less potential income you have. Many office supplies can readily be found at your local dollar or discount store.

Stock up when you find the items you need. Buy clear tape to attach shipping labels from your customers' e-mail, and brown tape for wrapping plain boxes. Padded envelopes are used to ship smaller, flat items. You can save some money shopping for these at discount stores.

STYROFOAM:
 Styrofoam can come in handy. I keep all the Styrofoam I receive from items I buy. Ask your friends to do the same for you. You will not use it very often but you will be happy you have it when it's needed. It is a great packing material to use to cushion china platters and plates. Sometimes you may actually be given a styrofoam box with a lid. These are great to package an expensive vase in. First I stuff the vase with clean paper, then I wrap it in bubble wrap. Next I put it in a cardboard box. Very delicate items will ship safely in this type of packaging. Customers will be happy to pay a few dollars more for the shipping, if it'll ensure safe arrival.

PLASTIC BAGS:
 Plastic store bags are very useful for garage sales. They also work adequately to wrap items.

NEWSPAPER:
 Newspaper is a good item to stuff some glass and pottery items for shipping. Hollow items need to be stuffed to stop vibrations that can crack glass or pottery. The U.S. Postal Service has a great information area on how to wrap items for shipment, **http://www.usps.com**. Newspaper is also a great product to wrap items at a garage sale or auction, for safe transportation of the items.

BUBBLE WRAP:
 Bubble wrap is the one item I buy. It is almost impossible to find it free of charge. I order it online in quantity. It can be a bit costly, so buy it in multiple rolls. Buying in large orders will save you some money on shipping costs. This is an absolutely necessary shipping item. Always have

additional stock on hand.

Bubble wrap comes in different sizes, and at various prices. You will find 3/16", 5/16" and 1/2" size bubbles. I buy all these sizes. They come with perforations at 12" or 24". This is helpful because you will not need to cut a piece. You just tear off the quantity you need. I find the 12" perforated bubble wrap the most useful. In addition, you can buy it in rolls of 62 feet, 125 feet, 250 feet or 300 feet long. Usually the larger the quantity purchased, the less expensive it becomes. You can also buy bubble wrap bags. They are great for jewelry. They also come in various sizes.

Make your friends, co-workers and family aware of your shipping material needs. If you are lucky, friends will give you the bubble wrap they receive from their own purchases. People love to recycle. It'll save you money in the long run and save them having to dispose of it. Buying it is easy. You may purchase it online. Auction sites auction incredible amounts of it. There are also individual shops online that sell shipping supplies. Personally, I buy mine on eBay. Try doing an ebay search for "bubble wrap". You will be amazed at your choices.

ACTUAL SHIPPING OF THE ITEM
I ship my "Good Junk" using the US Postal Service, **http://www.usps.com**. When an item sells, I box it and weigh it. As soon as I receive my customer's address, I log onto the postal site and use the postage calculation feature. You will need your customer's zip code to do this. It is very simple. The site is user friendly. After the price of shipping is determined, I e-mail my customer with a total due to me. This includes the item's cost, and shipping and insurance fees. A copy of the e-mail letter of

this transaction is attached to the outside of the box until the actual shipping day. When the payment is received, I cut out the shipping address from the e-mail letter and attach it to the box. I also complete an insurance slip and include it with the box for faster shipping. The box is either taken to the Post Office or put aside with a future shipping date noted on it. I try to ship most items U.S. Postal Service Priority whenever possible. I like to use the free box, tape and labels. If the item is very light or very heavy I will offer US Postal Service First Class or Parcel Post to save my customer some shipping costs. Take a virtual tour of their site. You will be very pleased. This is a real time saving site! There are other ways to ship your items. You may want to use UPS, **http://www.ups.com** or Federal Express, **http://www.federalexpress.com**. I suggest you look at all the options in your area. The more options you provide your customer with, the happier they will be.

PACKAGING TIPS

Do you have good packaging skills? If not, here are some great tips to help you ship items safely. Be sure to check with your shipping company. The Postal Service or UPS may have different requirements.

- **Use the right size box.**
- **Cushion items properly.**
- **Tape it up carefully.**
- **Good labeling is a must.**

Choosing the right size box
When choosing a box, be sure there is ample space on all sides. In this space, you will want to add cushioning material. After wrapping an item with good cushioning

material, try leaving a full inch all the way around the item. Boxes need to be strong enough to take a good fall. Corrugated boxes are ideal but next too impossible to find free. A box should be rigid and have full flaps. Make sure your box closes completely. If an item is very heavy, check your box to find out how much weight it can hold safely. This information is often on a bottom flap. Always remove old labels or addresses from a box. I have had an item shipped incorrectly because I missed removing a label.

Choosing the right cushioning materials

There are many good cushioning materials. Do not waste your bubble wrap on items that could use old newspaper. **Glassware, pottery and china** really do need bubble wrap. Always leave 3 inches around delicate items. Fill this space with packing peanuts or air pillows. Keep in mind that newspaper print comes off on some items. Never wrap opaque or frosted glassware in newspaper. Bubble wrap does not leave color behind. Always fill vases with clean paper to keep the vibrations at a minimum. Vibrations can crack your glass. I also like to use old styrofoam sheets to cushion plates and platters. I first wrap in a lighter bubble wrap, then I put foam on the top and bottom. Occasionally I find a styrofoam box with a lid. I keep these for very expensive glass or pottery items. I bubble wrap the item, put it in the styrofoam box and then box it again. They always arrive safely. Do not forget that double boxing can also work just fine. Providing a good one inch of packing peanuts around a glass item will usually insure good shipment.

Wooden items can be shipped safely with a good wrapping of newspaper. Tape lids closed. Never put the tape directly on the wood.

Metal objects do nicely with any paper wrapping. Very small items can be wrapped in tiny bubble wrap which is less expensive.

Art work or mirrors can be more difficult. First I paper wrap the item. Next I bubble wrap it. Styrofoam sheets are taped to the front and back of the item. The box I choose is usually very close to size of the frame. I then fill around it with packing peanuts. **Coins, stamps and jewelry** need to be put in boxes larger than the item. Very small boxes are likely to come up missing. When shipping jewelry, wrap each piece in its own bubble wrap bag so they do not rub against each other.

When shipping items together, wrap each item in bubble wrap, then leave space between them. Be very careful in stacking them against each other. This can result in damage.

Items that are **liquid,** like **perfume,** need extra careful packing. Wrap these in a plastic bag after carefully wrapping in plain paper. Put a lot of bubble wrap and peanuts in the box.

If you hear any rattling, you need to add more cushioning to the box.

Measuring your box

Shipping rates can vary by box size in addition to weight. The terms you will see are length, and girth. **Length** is the longest side of the box. **Girth** is the distance all the way around the package at its widest point perpendicular to the length. Shipping companies may vary on accepted sizes. If you are not sure of an item, check on the company policies prior to running your item's listing.

International shipping

Some sellers prefer to not ship internationally. I ship all over the world. Limiting yourself to only the U.S. and Canada is very shortsighted. Some items will attract more bidding when international sales are accepted. I will agree there is a bit more work involved. You cannot memorize shipping rates out of the country. There are more shipping methods available. Some methods do not allow insurance. I find mailing these items using the U.S. Postal Service is quite easy. I use their postage calculator and I remind my customers that insuring overseas shipments is very costly. This is where exceptional wrapping skills pay off. You need to be doubly careful. I, personally, have had no lost overseas packages or broken goods. It is also very handy to develop a good working relationship with your postmaster or postal clerk. These individuals can be very helpful. International shipping does require a customs form. They are easy to fill out.

Insurance

Some carriers automatically insure your items up to $100. of item value. Others charge a fee. These charges are paid by your customer. Encourage them to pay the fee. It is usually less than $2.50. If the item is not packaged properly, the company may not pay the damaged goods claim.

Choosing the right tape

Never use masking tape. It does not hold up well. Try buying pressure sensitive plastic tape or use the Priority tape that the Postal Service provides. I find a good plastic tape works well. I also like to cover my labels with a clear tape. Do not scrimp on tape. Use enough to securely close the package.

Odd shaped items
Some items are incredibly difficult to wrap. You may need to combine boxes or reshape boxes to get the right size. Be sure to tape these heavily. The item inside may need extra padding or support. Always position an item in the center of a box. If it is hollow, fill the inside with paper. I have shipped very large plant stands and floor lamps very successfully. Be very creative. Some companies will allow an item to be shipped without a box. Do this only for items that cannot be easily scratched.

Electronic equipment
Be careful in this area. Some items need anti-static packing materials! Use factory original packing boxes if possible.

Always package items carefully. Take your time and encourage customers to pay the little extra that insurance costs.

CHAPTER 10: What If Your Item Does Not Sell, or...Oops, I Bought REAL Junk!

Some items just do not sell, despite your best efforts. You try your favorite online auction, try lesser popular auction sites, change online auction categories, change your description, even put it in your web store for a few weeks. Nothing works! It just will not sell. "Oops, you may have bought REAL junk!" or maybe you miscalculated its value or appeal. This happens to all of us. The ultimate goal is to recover the money you paid for it. Your question when buying an item should always be, "Can I get my money back on this?" Usually you can. But sometimes it takes a bit more work than you anticipated.

What do you do now? Do not get discouraged. There are other options to be considered. Try having a yearly garage sale to liquidate your poor buys. These sales are best during your community village-wide sale days. Price the item to sell. Keep in mind that you need to recapture this lost money in order to buy new inventory. When necessary, lose a little money on these items. Just get them sold.

Another idea is to use some purchases as gifts, but **ONLY** if your friend or family member likes "Good Junk." Do not insult the people who still think you are selling **REAL** junk!

Another idea is to try local auction houses that specialize

in auctioning estate auctions. They will charge you a small percentage of the total sales to auction box lots for you. This can bring some unexpected income. Occasionally you can make great money using their services. Look in your telephone directory for a list of your local auctioneers. Do not let some bad purchases discourage you. Everyone has these. Look ahead to your next buying trip!

CHAPTER 11: What Is Good Customer Service?

Good customer service is the same, whether you sell online, or in a brick and mortar store. People like to feel important and respected when they are spending their money. They want to feel they are number one, the only customer you have at the moment. This can be very challenging when you are dealing with an upset customer, another who has questions about an item in your web store, 20 e-Bay auctions ending, your grandson's ill and you need to be ready to go hiking in one hour! How **DO** you make everyone happy?

First you must learn that you cannot make everyone happy. You will have an occasional customer that is unreasonable. You will not be able to satisfy her or him. After realizing you are not going to have a perfect record, you can strive to be very good at customer service. You will need to decide which customers need immediate attention. Tackle one task or problem at a time and set aside any problems that can be dealt with tomorrow.

To provide good customer service you need to make your customer aware of how you ship, when you ship and the payments you accept . They will want to know your item return policy. Nothing should be left to his or her imagination. They need a lot of information and reassurance that you are a professional seller. Be prompt with e-mails and honest at all times.
  Make a realistic selling plan and work the plan!

Include below are some ideas to help you provide good customer service.

Pre-planned E-mail

Use preplanned e-mail whenever possible. These can be used to contact customers after an auction has closed or to provide the final item amount due to you. There is no reason to repeatedly retype the same message to your customers. I keep a Word Perfect file of some basic e-mail that I can copy and paste into a customer's e-mail. These shortcuts will save you time. Try setting up your own preplanned e-mail such as:

#1. "HI - Thanks for ordering from me! Your total is $ _____. It will be sent USPS Priority and insured. I accept PayPal, Payingfast, Yahoo Pay Direct, Bidpay, money orders and checks. Items paid by check are held approximately seven days until your check clears my bank . All others will ship the next or same day! Thank you again. Please send your payment to:
Your name
Your address.

#2. "Hi - You are my winning bid! Thank you. Please send me your address, including a zip code. I'll get back to you with a shipping amount and a total."
Your name
Your address

#3. "Hi - Your payment has been received. Thank you. I'll ship your item on ....".
Your name
Your address."

#4. "Hi - This is a friendly reminder. I have not received

your payment for the item you purchased from me on
_____. Please advise me on the status of your
payment. Thank you.
>Your name
>Your address."

#5. "Hi - I am still holding your item ,........., from my web
store. I have not received your payment. Other customers
are expressing an interest in it. Please advise me regarding
the status of this transaction. Thank you."
>Your name
>Your address.

Other notification methods
Other notification methods can save you valuable time.
PayPal, **www.paypal.com**, has a customer notification
system. It is currently free with your business account.
This feature can streamline your business and will save
you time. You are able to customize the messages. When
an auction closes, they send an automatic notification for
you! See their site for details regarding setting up a
business account and the free notification feature.

Vacation notifications
When you anticipate being on vacation or away from your
computer for a long period of time, add these vacation
dates to your e-mail or PayPal notifications. Customers
get nervous if an auction ends and you are not responding
to their e-mail. Try to avoid having your auctions end
while you are unavailable. Arrange your listing dates to
end when you are home and available. You can also try
using ten day auctions versus the seven day ones, to
accommodate your extended trip.

Follow up within 24 hours or less after the auction

closes

Always follow up with your customer very quickly after an auction closes. The faster you contact a customer, the better they like it. I try to contact customers within 24 hours or less.

Use a Priority package delivery service whenever possible

Whenever it is possible, use a Priority Mail service if it's economical for the customer. Priority packages arrives most anywhere in the country within 2-3 days. I use the U.S. Postal Mail service. Deliveries are often in two days. These packages also look very professional. Try to ship the same day or the next day if a customer pays with a service like PayPal or with a money order. Items paid by personal checks should be shipped as soon as they clear your bank. Do not make a customer wait for a convenient shipping day for you. Your customer should be your number one priority!

Customers DO rate your service on quickness of delivery.

Be honest

Honesty in descriptions is of utmost importance. Always be very accurate. List all the items' flaws. Don't pretend you know where it originated from or who manufactured it if you do not know. Be honest regarding estimating shipping costs. Never overcharge for shipping. If you feel you must add a handling fee, put that in your description. Don't surprise your customer. Try to always build the cost of doing business into your opening bid or the price you charge in your web store. Being dishonest will always result in a poor reputation, cause customer complaints and eventually adversely affect your sales.

Keep a customer "want" list

When a customer requests an item that you do not have in stock, keep a file of these requested items. A customer want list is a valuable tool. It provides you with the opportunity to keep in touch with customers. When you buy an item they have previously asked for, you can contact them to see if they are still looking for it. Even if they aren't, they will see your web store site noted in your e-mail correspondence. They may take a second look at your site and see something they would like to purchase!

Cash checks quickly
Banking on a regular basis makes good sense. Cash your customer checks daily. You should make banking a regular stop on your way home from work. Do not hold customer checks. This can slow down the shipping of customer items. This results in poor customer service.

Clean up / Polish up
Clean up the items you are selling. Not only do customers appreciate it but it almost always brings you a higher selling price. Be careful not to destroy the natural patina of some metals. Some metals develop a dark appearance over time. I do not always clean brass or silver. Generally speaking, you should sell items as you find them. Some items may need a light cleaning to show details, but proceed very carefully. Cleaning can cause additional wear to the metal. Glass items always need cleaning. Nothing looks worse in a picture than fingerprints and dirt. I use a general dish detergent for most items. Do keep in mind, some paint was applied without firing {baking it on}, it may wash right off!

I remember my first big cleaning mistake. I soaked a painted cat figurine in a harsh soapy water mixture. Thirty minutes later, I found a cat with no paint on it at all! The item no longer had any resale value. Do not scrub painted merchandise. Fabrics should have stains removed, but only if you can do so without damaging the piece. Wooden items should be washed and dried. I use wood polish and oils sparingly. When in doubt, do nothing.

Provide feedback

Feedback is another valuable tool. Most online auction sites have an area to provide feedback, a customer or seller's opinion of the transaction. Always provide your customer with positive feedback. Positive feedback is always welcome. When providing negative feedback, it should state facts only. Emotion should stay of it. Statements like "Payment has never been received by this dealer", is factual. Insults are unwarranted and can be damaging to you in the end. Negative comments can upset your customer and cause him/her to retaliate. Be very slow in providing negative feedback. Negative feedback can backfire and waste valuable selling time. Always try to resolve customer problems quickly.

Customers look at feedback as your selling reputation. It gives them a sense of whom they are dealing with. Good seller feedback can increase your sales. Keep in mind that many customers will not provide you feedback if you do not provide it for them. I like to use some standard feedback messages. These I keep in a Word file and I cut and paste them into the feedback form. When using eBay's feedback system, go to their toolbar at the top of any eBay page. Look for "feedback forum" and click on it. A list of choices will be available. Click on an area named "leave feedback about a user-see all pending comments at once." In this area, you will have the opportunity to see everyone you have not left feedback for. Feedback for everyone can be completed on this page. It is a terrific way to save time. Try using statements such as "All around smooth transaction. A++ customer" or " Easy, fast - a real eBay asset. A++". Just keep in mind, the faster you complete it, the faster they will post feedback for you.

Respond to all customer complaints quickly

Answer customer complaints quickly and politely, even if you feel the customer may be wrong. You need to use good judgment regarding refunds. Often you will do better to accept customer returns and resell the items. You can avoid many customer complaints by being very honest in your item descriptions. I have found that most customer complaints could have been avoided if I had done something differently in the first place. Always resolve the conflict. Negative feedback will definitely affect your online sales. You **will** lose money.

Keep insurance receipts

Keep the insurance shipping receipts. You will occasion-ally need one. They are needed for customers who have received broken merchandise. A sales receipt and the postal insurance receipt are needed for the customer to start her/his complaint with the Postal Service. Good packing can help insure against broken items. Despite your best efforts there will be a broken item at some time in your selling career. Hopefully you will only have a couple of them every year. To save yourself time, have the receipts readily available. When a customer asks to not insure an item, I keep a copy of that e-mail. It's also a good idea to keep a dated general receipt from the shipping agent. This is also true for all international shipments.

Always treat your customer the way you like would to be treated by a business. Be honest, efficient, and friendly.

Consider all customer requests for refunds. Be prompt in providing feedback. Good customer service will increase your sales, improve repeat customer orders and build up your reputation as a competent and professional business person.

A Customer's Viewpoint

I recently received an interesting e-mail from a slightly unhappy customer. She had won a few bids on a popular auction site and was frustrated with the difference in sellers approaches for requesting payment. I found this e-mail very enlightening, enough so that I reevaluated my part in her confusion. A portion of her letter read as follows; " buying items on .... has become too complex. Some people immediately send a total due; some get your shipping address and then send the total; some take PayPal; some don't; some automatically link you to a payment site; some don't; some do the .... automatic checkout and some sellers say do not do the automatic checkout; it goes on and on."

She continues by stating; "I made eleven purchases on .... this week and I'm tearing my hair out: I think the time has come that some kind of uniformity has to come about for .... to continue, because quite frankly, I'm beginning to find it to be more trouble than it's worth." She went on to explain her frustration and was apologetic for taking it out on me. I found this customer's complaint useful. We should always be looking at new ways to provide better customer service. Obviously, many customers want simple, and direct transactions. Our effort's goal should be directed toward how we can simplify the whole online auction experience to make it more user-friendly.

CHAPTER 12: Do You Know What a Duck Is?

My duck theory:

If it walks like a duck, looks like a duck and quacks like a duck.....then it's probably a duck!

This holds true in buying merchandise. Does it look too perfect? Does the shop have three of these items for sale? If so, it may be a reproduction . . . a great copy of an older piece. Or perhaps it may be an expertly repaired item. Look for signs of age. Scratches on the bottom or some minor roughness on glass edges indicate some age. If there are no signs of age, be wary. Be alert and observant. A small chip, or a reproduction, will often greatly alter your selling price.

But keep in mind, ducks can sell well! Your customer needs to know it may be reproduction or that it may have been repaired. Be honest about every aspect of your knowledge of the item, the exact condition of the item and any professional opinion you may have about the item. Unhappy customers and returned goods will cost you money.

CHAPTER 13: I'm Not Good at Buying "Good Junk"! What Can I Do to Make Money?

You hate the hunt for " Good Junk" but love the antiquing world and wonder what can you can do to make money. If you really enjoy your computer and enjoy the antique dealers, why not be an auction lister? An auction lister sets up auctions or items for sale online for other dealers. Some dealers really dislike computers or do not have the time to devote to an online business. Other sellers want the human contact that a brick and mortar shop provides. If you enjoy the online world and want to work at home, money can be made, selling "Good Junk" for others. Dealers will pay you a commission to sell items for them. You can sell on the online auctions or you can set up a store front like **http://www. Cyberattic.com**.

Your equipment needs and organizational skills will remain the same. You must decide if you will do the shipping or have the dealer do it. Personally I like the control of handling the complete sale myself. Your reputation as a seller may be compromised if the owner of the merchandise does not follow through on shipping in a timely fashion.

Most antique dealers will write a description of the item for you. This is handy if you are unfamiliar with the item he or she has you selling. If you are a good description writer and knowledgeable in the "Good Junk" business, you can make larger commissions by adding this service to your repertoire.

Commissions can vary greatly. The more services you do for the dealer, the more you can charge him or her. The dealer should pay you a commission and the fees incurred in selling this item. The commission should be based on the selling price. Most auction listers charge 10-50% of the selling price. If all fees are paid by the seller, in my opinion, a 20% commission is fair. You may want to accept only high-end goods. These items will sell for more money and make you a larger commission.

I have sold a few really great items for other dealers and made a tidy profit. I listed a 1950's Elvis Presley bubble gum card set for $1000. on my **Cyberattic.com** store. The commission was $150.00. I had three hours work in it. That's a nice profit. A fishing reel I sold on eBay for a friend sold for $750. We split the profit. I earned $200.00 for that transaction.

Some of us combine selling for others with our own business transactions. When selling for others, choose the items carefully. Avoid selling very small priced items unless you get the feeling it may be an exceptional item.

The definite advantage of selling for others is, you have no money tied up in inventory. Be very careful to choose people you can trust. Always put your verbal agreement of commissions and fees in a written form . You need to have a contract indicating that your income on these sales is only the commission.

In conclusion, you can make money selling for others. Set this up as a business and utilize good organizational skills.

CHAPTER 14: What Do You Do If ...Your Customer Does Not Pay You?

In every business there is a chance that your customer will not pay his bill. Online auctions pose the same problem. On occasion, a winning bidder will not contact you nor respond to your winning bid notification. So what do you do now? What are your options? How do you collect your money? That depends on where you are selling your product. Auction sites do address the problem of non-paying bidders. A bid is a contract between you and the customer. Procedures vary somewhat. If you are selling on your own web site store front, it's a totally different process.

First of all, do not immediately think your high bidder on an auction site is a deadbeat customer. Some just respond slower. Your high bidder may not be able to respond to you right away for legitimate reasons. A customer may be out of town on business or on vacation. Illness or a death in the family is a possible reason to not respond. Proceed cautiously. Do not become accusing or irate.

Most online auctions have a non-paying bidder policy. eBays' policies are great. I find them quite effective in deterring deadbeat customers. You will start the procedure on eBays' home page. You will find an area called "services" on the tool bar. You will click on this and proceed into"buying and selling." Your next step is to click on "request final value fee credit." This is the area to learn about eBays' "non-paying bidder" program. eBay lists three occurrences. Each one has a warning. Currently, on the third warning the non-payer is indefinitely suspended.

Most auctions expect the customer and seller to contact each other within three days. After three days, but not past thirty days, if your customer has not contacted you, you may start a formal complaint. This first step involves sending a "reminder notice." You can use the auction site's notice or compose your own. Then you will wait seven days. If the customer does not respond or has not paid his bill, your next step is filing a formal complaint. This is called a "Non-Paying Bidder Alert Form." eBay contacts them and encourages them to pay you. You must fill it out within thirty days of the auction's closing date. The bidder has ten days to respond to the alert. Once the alert is filed, you may stop holding the item for the customer. After the ten days passes, you should complete the last step of requesting the "refund of your final value fee." It is at this point that eBay will refund your fee to your account.

This may sound a bit complicated, but it really is not. eBay has the procedure in one area of their site and it is easy to follow. I have had to do this only a few times in five years. The most amazing phenomenon is, my item often sells better the next time around! You also have the option of offering the item to your under bidder of the original auction. eBay calls it "second chance." They explain that on the same page with the full non-paying bidder program. I usually just re-list my item and start fresh.

After I've completed the full policy procedure, I post negative "feedback" and use the " block bidder" feature. The block bidder feature blocks the deadbeat customer from bidding on your auctions again.

If you resolve the problem with your customer after you have completed the non paying bidder program, eBay also outlines how to retract the complaint. Once negative feedback is posted, it really does damage a buyer or seller's reputation. Again I advise you to proceed very carefully when thinking of using this feature.

If selling on a web store, you can only use reminders to encourage your customer to pay. I offer PayPal as a paying service. Often customers will send the money immediately. If a customer waits to send a check or money order the risk of non payment goes up. If a customer does not send payment, I send a note called "friendly reminder." In this note I remind the customer that I'm holding an item and losing any potential sale. I ask them to please advise me on their intentions regarding this sale. Unfortunately you will encounter "non payers" a bit more frequently. These potential sales are lost to you. You have no recourse but to sell to the next customer who inquires. I always leave my item available on my **Cyberattic.com** site until I receive payment. If a new request comes in, I advise the new customer that I have a potential sale but will contact them if it falls through. I allow 10 days for payment to be received. If it's an out of the country sale, these can take three weeks to complete.

In conclusion, selling is not always without its problems. You must expect to encounter the deadbeat customer at times. Do expect most customers to pay timely. Treat slower paying customers with respect. When a sale falls though, just follow the procedures in place and continue along with your plan.

CHAPTER 15: Security and Safety Online

You now know where to buy your goods and how to sell them. You can see how the auction world can benefit you as a seller and as a buyer. If you are like many people, you will be spending a lot of time online. The Internet has so much to offer. There are great places to sell, buy and research items. You can conduct almost all your banking online. You can buy the most common items you need. But you must also know there are unsavory characters out there. There is the potential for your personal information to be seen by the wrong people. You need to take much care in your online activities. In this chapter, I will give you a "crash course" in online safety and security.

When I discuss safety on the Internet with friends and family, I like to put this in perspective. You can easily get ripped off in a local store or on the telephone. Most of us use ATM machines without any concern. Every day we give our credit card numbers or bank account numbers to a salesperson or a waiter or waitress. We don't know these people. We trust that the stores and businesses we deal with employ trustworthy employees. That's false security! We can get ripped off quite easily but we do it anyway. Luckily, we seldom if ever, get our information stolen. I feel the same way about the Internet. It can happen but does not happen as often as we might think.

Personally I do not know anyone who has had any major problems using the Internet. Yes, occasionally someone complains about an online purchase. Usually they did not do enough to investigate the seller prior to bidding on an auction or they ordered from an unknown online store. I know people who avoid using the Internet and they still had their checking account used by someone else. I have known individuals who had their credit cards stolen. So in conclusion do not be afraid to transact business online, just follow some good safety procedures. Many of these are just basic, good common sense ideas.

- Don't buy from online businesses that you have never heard of before. Research the site first. Ask friends if they ever ordered from the company. Place orders with companies that also have brick and mortar stores. Some great examples are J.C.Penneys, Walmart, and L.L.Bean.

- Be sure the site has security measures in place. You will find an icon of a lock on their page if they are protected. Do not use sites that are unprotected.

- When using online banking, set your computer up with a 128 bit encryption security measure. This is designed to protect and secure the personal-data privacy of individual users. This program is often found free and is simple to download on your computer. Try looking at **www.pcworld.com**, under "downloads," "privacy and encryption." In this area, as of this date, you will find a free 128 bit download file.

- Never give out any personal or credit information via your e-mail system.

- When using online auction sites, review the sellers "feedback." Take other buyers' comments seriously when deciding to buy from an individual.

■ Use credit cards or third party payment services like PayPal to purchase your item online. These services have built in protection against unsatisfactory purchases.

■ Consider installing a " firewall" on your computer. A firewall is a set of programs residing on a gateway server that protects your computer from an outside network. It regulates traffic coming into your computer and can protect you from outside electronic attacks. They can stop outside networks from viewing your sensitive information. You can read up on these programs by doing a general online search and typing in "firewall definition." It is rather difficult to understand. I personally tried one and felt it slowed down my computer too much. Other people have used them and were very pleased. You will need to determine your individual need for this type of protection.

My conclusion regarding safety and security online is to approach online buying very much like shopping in the real world. Always know to whom you are giving your sensitive information. Keep your account numbers in a safe place. Don't give out account numbers via e-mail. Use a common sense approach to Internet buying and you will eliminate a great deal of potential problems.

CHAPTER 16: My Favorite Web Sites

Over the past seven years I have found many terrific and useful web sites. All of them can provide you with valuable information. We can all benefit from great resources.
I use guidebooks but also enjoy online research.

Andale.com is described as an online service that helps manage all aspects of your auction process. It provides many services to the online auction seller. It's greatest service for me has been picture or image hosting. They also have counters, and listing of auction items. You can find their services and price structure at **http://www.andale.com**

Amazon has been best known as an online bookstore. They also have an auction site. They also allow you to list and sell used books. This is a great place to research used book prices and to sell yours. You will also find web stores on this web site. **http://www.amazon.com**

Bidpay is a third party online payment service. This is a Western Union company. They allow customers to send you money via wire or with a money order. The money order is mailed directly to you. It will arrive in approximately one week. **http://www.bidpay.com**

Brimfield Antique Show is located yearly in Massachusetts. This web site provides all the information you can want regarding the show. It is the largest outdoor show in New England. They have five thousand dealers from all around the country. This is an incredible experience. **http://www.brimfield.com**

C.A.D. Collecters and Dealers is described as software designed for the collector and the dealers. You can list inventory, track expenses and print reports and labels. The cost is really quite minimal for the wonderful features it provides. This is an affordable alternative to keeping handwritten records. You can find them at **http://tinkerware.com**.

California Country is an Antique Show and Sale in Los Altos, California. There are fifty dealers selling wonderful country Antiques of high quality. This show is held in October. For details visit their web site at **http://www.californiacountryshow.com**

Corridor 127 is called "The World's Longest Outdoor Garage Sale". It runs 450 miles down Corridor 127. This is THE event for garage sale enthusiasts. It's running through Tennessee, Kentucky and Alabama. **http://www.bargain-mall.com/127cor/index.htm**

Cyberattic.com is in my opinion the prime web store selling site for good junk and collectibles on the Internet. It is an affordable, easy to use and profitable web store front. Visit them at **http:www.cyberattic.com**

eBay. Who has not heard of this auction site? eBay, in my opinion, still remains the best online auction site. It is easy, fun and profitable. They can provide you with many of the services needed to run your online auction business. In addition they have built a sense of community and a great networking system. Do take a serious look at them. **http://www.ebay.com**

Fleamarket guide is a web site listing flea markets in the United States. This is a terrific resource for traveling. **http://www.fleamarketguide.com**

Localyardsales.com is a Canadian web site to list your yard sales.
You can list your sale or find sales in your area. Quite an interesting web site. If you live or shop in Canada, it's worth a peek.
http://www.localyardsales.com

PayPal is a third party online payment service that accepts your customers credit cards and checks. They deposit the money directly into your bank account. The seller pays a small fee based on the transaction amount.
http://www.paypal.com

PayDirect is Yahoo auction site's online third party payment service that accepts your customers credit cards and checks. They deposit the money directly into your bank account. The seller pays a small fee based on the transaction amount **http://www.auctions.yahoo.com**

Replacements.com is a wonderful site to buy, or use to research, china patterns. **http://www.replacements.com**

Sunday Driver is a terrific regional guide to Antique shops in New York State, Commonwealth of Virginia, and State of North Carolina. I love the maps and precise directions this site provides. They also have brochures available. **http://www.sundaydriver.com**

Libbey.com is a wonderful site to research Syracuse china or Libbey glass. This is an interesting web site. **http://www.libbey.com**

Tias is a great site to buy or sell Antiques and collectibles. It's also a nice area to research item prices. It is an online multi-dealer shop.
http://www.tias.com

United States Postal Service {U.S.P.S.} is my favorite site for calculating postal shipping rates, reading up on great tips about packaging items to ship and for ordering shipping supplies. This is a very easy to use site filled with great information, **http://www.usps.com**.

UPS is another way to ship your customer's items. This site is easy to use.
http://www.ups.com

World's Largest Garage Sale is in Warrensburg, NY every October. This is a super place to pick "Good Junk" and see the beautiful colorful leaves of Autumn. The entire town has garage sales. Antique dealers also have some great booths set up. Local shops are open. There are more than one thousand vendors. For details and directions visit their online web site at **http://www.warrensburggaragesale.com**.

Yard Sales Supplies.com is an interesting, comprehensive site for people who love garage sales. You can purchase your yard sale supplies here. They also have links to finding garage sales.
http://www.protoquest.com/YSS/Resources/FleaMark ets/locations.cgi

Yahoo auction is one of the nicest online auction sites. They have reasonable fees, lots of goods up for auction and interesting resource areas. They also have individual shops. Also of interest is their payment service PayDirect. You will find them at:

http://www.auctions.yahoo.com

CHAPTER 17: My Favorite Reference Sources

Resource and reference materials are very important. When learning the "Good Junk" business, you need to be able to identify the goods out there. Not everything you need to research is in a book or a price guide, but there is an incredible amount you can find easily. I keep a small reference library in my home. This is more for identification of an item than actual pricing. Prices in collector books are for items in mint condition. When selling online, especially at an auction, book price is really not that important. The books provide you with information regarding reproductions and show pictures. Listed below are my favorite books. This is not a comprehensive listing of guidebooks available. You will find more books in your local book store or online.

Books:

Florence's Glassware Pattern Identification Guide. *By Gene Florence. Collector Books, a Division of Schroeder Publishing Co. Inc. Paducah, Kentucky*
This book provides easy identification of glassware from the 1920's through the 1960's . It has wonderful pictures that make identification of patterns easy.

An Illustrated Value Guide to Cookie Jars *by Erma-gene Westfall.Collector Books, Paducah, Kentucky.*

This is a terrific book, with colorful pictures, and it lists different manufacturers.

Pyrex By Corning A Collector's Guide *by Susan Tobier Rogove; Marcia Buan Steinhauer: Antique Publications, Marietta, Ohio.*
I love this book. It provides a history of Pyrex glassware. The pictures are great for identification. This is a great resource.

Anchor Hocking's Fire King & More. Identification & Value Guide Including Early American Prescut and Wexford *by Gene Florence: Collector's Books, a Division of Schroeder Publishing Co. Inc. Paducah, Kentucky*
This book is a wonderful, comprehensive picture and price guide. This is a very nice resource for identification of unusual pieces.

Collectible Glassware from 40's, 50's, 60's... *By Gene Florence: Collector books, a Division of Schroeder Publishing Co. Inc. Paducah, Kentucky*
This book is an illustrated price guide with a lot of colorful pictures and many different manufacturers.

Elegant Glassware of the Depression Era *by Gene Florence: Collector books, a Division of Schroeder Publishing Co. Inc. Paducah, Kentucky*
This book is a terrific book, with colorful pictures, listing many manufacturers.

100 Years of Collectible Jewelry (1850-1950), *by Lillian Baker; Collector books, a Division of Schroeder Publishing co. Inc. Paducah, Kentucky*
This book has a delightful introduction to eras of jewelry manufacturing and a chapter "All about Jewelry." You will find a lot of great pictures.

Wallace-Homestead Price Guide to American Country Antiques *by Don & Carol Raycraft; Wallace-Homestead, a division of Chilton Book Company.*
A book just filled with many colorful pictures. It lists many wonderful kitchen and primitive items. You will find a chapter on reproductions and fakes. This is a nice all around reference book.

Garage Sale & Flea Market Annual *by Schroeder Publishing Co. Paducah, Kentucky.*
503 pages filled with common items you can find at garage sales and flea markets. A really great resource for the garage sale addict!

Kitchen Antiques with Values *by Frances Johnson. Schiffer Publishing Ltd. Atglen, PA.*
This is a fabulous book full of splatter ware, kitchen mixers, grinders and general merchandise. This book is a must!

Standard Encylopedia of Carnival Glass 6th Edition *by Bill Edwards, Mike Carwile. Collector books, a Division of Schroeder Publishing co. Inc. Paducah, Kentucky*

This book has an interesting array of carnival glass. Colorful pictures and a price guide will delight you.

A Collector's Guide to Candy Containers Identification and Values *by Douglas M. Dezso, J. Leon Poirier, Rose D. Poirier. Collector books, a Division of Schroeder Publishing co. Inc. Paducah, Kentucky*
You will find a fun and informative guide to candy containers. This book is colorful and a needed reference source for "Good Junk" buyers.

A Collector's Guide to Porcelier China Identification and Values *By Susan E. Grindberg. Collector books, a Division of Schroeder Publishing co. Inc. Paducah, Kentucky.*
This book includes some company history and terrific pictures. This guide has great old lighting fixtures, in addition to china.

Crackle Glass Identification and Value Guide. Book II. *By Stan &Arlene Weitman. Collector books, a Division of Schroeder Publishing co. Inc. Paducah, Kentucky*
This book has an incredible amount of crackle glass pictured. The book is interesting and informative. A great reference guide for buyers and sellers alike.

Antiquing magazines/newspapers:

Antiques & Auction News *published by Joel Sater Publications. Mount Joy. PA*
This is my favorite newspaper. It is published weekly and is available at hundreds of shows, markets, auctions, shops and centers. You will find Auction listings from all

over the East coast. There are informative articles on Antiques. It advertises Antique shows and has a classified section. This is an all around great publication.

There are other publications available throughout the country and in Canada. Ask your local auctioneers or antique shops which are available in your area.

Online collector clubs:

Clarice Cliff Collectors Club is a collectors' site for this pottery line. This site is great to view pictures, research current prices and join in a chat with other collectors. **http://www.claricecliff.com**

Coca -A-Cola Collectors Club. This club describes itself as a non-profit club for collectors who are interested in the history and the collection of vintage and new Coca -A -Cola company **memorabilia.** There is a lot of interesting information. You can buy and sell coke items on this site. It's worth a look. **http://cocacolaclub.org**

Fiesta Collectors Club. This site is self-described as the original Fiesta Collector's Club. It also includes other china lines. There are fabulous, colorful pictures. They include a lot of information regarding patterns. Price lists are available via regular mail. You can join their newsletter. A wonderful, fun site. **http://www.chinaspecialties.com/fiesta.html**

There are many online collectors' clubs. Try doing a general search via a search engine like Yahoo. Type in your item and you will certainly find a club online. Clubs can help you identify rare pieces or learn pricing.

Online searches:
Try a "completed item" search on any Auction site. This will give you current online prices. You will also find interesting information regarding sizes and colors of similar pieces.

eBay, Yahoo, Cyberattic.com: These web sites have great informational areas on their web sites. You will find articles and general information. They are great reference sources. Don't overlook them.
http://www.paypal.com
http://www.auctions.yahoo.com
http://www.cyberattic.com

CONCLUSION

You now have the basic and common sense tools to turn your hobby into a profitable business. You can name your income. You CAN make money selling "Good Junk"! All it requires is the willingness to work hard ... to take a risk......to step outside the box....and start to leave your comfort zone. Start big or start small .....just start. It will serve you well, whatever your goal.

Contact me if I can help you. You can contact me through my web store, Linda's Little House at
http://www.cyberattic.com,
or e-mail me at *lovely13675@usadatanet.net*

APPENDIX I: Basics of Good Customer Service

- Accurate shipping costs

- Careful packaging of items

- Clean merchandise

- Customer want list

- Efficient handling of customer complaints and refunds.

- Feedback on sales

- Honesty

- Organized business practices

- Prompt e-mail and notification of winning bids and customer payments

- Timely response to questions

APPENDIX II: GENERAL TERMS

BIDPAY - Online third party payment service that accepts money orders from your customer and mails them to you. They charge the buyer a fee.

BEST PRICE- The least amount of money a seller will accept for an item.

BOOK PRICE- The price found in a Collectors guide book. These are written by experts from a particular collecting field.

C.A.D. - Computer software program that allows you to list inventory and business expenses.

COST OF DOING BUSINESS- Includes the amount of money paid for an item, any shipping cost paid, and overhead costs to run your business.

CYBERATTIC.COM - Cyberattic.com is a group of online web stores. They sell antiques, collectibles and much more.

DUCK - A duck is a possible reproduction of an older item, or a repaired piece.

"GOOD JUNK"- My term for ordinary, everyday items that have resale potential.

FEED BACK - Customer and seller's online rating

system of an auction transaction. Feedback is completed for sellers and buyers on online auction sites.

IMAGE HOSTING - A web site that holds your item pictures until you list them on an auction or in a web store.

ISP - These are your Internet providers, such as AOL

PICKING - Picking means looking for items to sell.

PAYPAL -Online third party payment service that accepts your customers credit cards and checks. They deposit the money directly into your bank account. The seller pays a small fee based on the transaction amount.

PAY DIRECT - Yahoo auction sites' online third party payment service that accepts your customers credit cards and checks. They deposit the money in your bank account. The seller pays a small fee based on the transaction amount.

PIE BIRD- A little figurine used to allow steam to escape from a pie while it bakes.

SET PRICE - The price you decide to sell an item for on a web store. Customers do not bid.

SMALLS- Refers to items sold that are easy to ship. They are not usually furniture.

VINTAGE- A vintage piece is not an antique but definitely is an older item.

APPENDIX III: CHECKLIST OF OFFICE SUPPLIES

- Computer printer paper
- Envelopes
- Floppy disks
- Ink cartridges for a printer
- Measuring tape
- Magnifying glass
- Notebooks
- Paper clips
- Pens; blue, red, black
- Pencils
- Postal customs slips
- Postal insurance forms (from your local post office)
- Sales receipt book
- Stamps
- Stapler

INDEX

Lightning Source UK Ltd.
Milton Keynes UK
UKOW04f120170515

251686UK00001B/12/P

9 781589 393592